FIGURING
OUT THE FED

**Answers to the most frequently asked questions
about the Federal Reserve System**

Compiled by Margaret Thoren

April, 1993

First printing March, 1985
Second printing June, 1985
Third printing March, 1986
Revised Second Edition April, 1993

Library of Congress Catalog Card Number 93-60047
ISBN 0-9606938-6-6
SAN 219-8266

Desktop Publishing by David Faroo, Valley Publishing
Graphic Design by Marino Puhalj

Truth In Money, Inc.
P. O. Box 30
Chagrin Falls, Ohio 44022

Printed in the United States of America

Foreword

If you've ever had even a passing interest in how the Federal Reserve *really* works, but didn't want to spend time in the library finding out, this book is for you.

It answers basic questions like: "Are the 12 regional Federal Reserve Banks privately-owned corporations?" (Question #12). And it answers tough questions like: "Where does the Federal Reserve get the money it uses to buy government bonds?" (Question #46).

Total debt — Federal debt plus private sector debt — in the country is now around $16 trillion, which is over two and a half times the value of all the goods and services we create in a year (the so-called gross domestic product, or GDP). Compound interest causes the debt to grow as the clock ticks. In the time it will take you to read this book, the Federal debt alone will have increased $40,000,000.

There is a direct link between debt growth and the mechanics of the money system administered by the Federal Reserve. So, if we want to solve the debt problem in the country, we first have to understand how the Fed operates. And with the Federal debt growing at $40 million dollars an hour, there isn't a whole lot of time to figure out the Fed before the national economy self-destructs.

Figuring out the Fed puts answers at your fingertips. It is the companion to *The Truth In Money Book* which contains detailed information about what is wrong with the money system — and how to fix it.

Introduction

Most traditional economics textbooks give the impression that public sector debt, and interest on this debt, have little impact on economic conditions. Many textbooks teach that public sector debt has little or no effect on the world around us because, they say, we owe this debt "to ourselves."

If "we" owe this massive, multi-trillion dollar debt to "ourselves," why don't "we" just forgive "ourselves" and start over again?

We can't, and we don't, because the lion's share of the Federal debt is owed by the government to financial institutions — including the multi-national banks, the twelve regional Federal Reserve Banks, foreign governments and foreign institutions. The government goes into debt and we, the taxpayers, ultimately bear the responsibility for repaying these obligations, plus interest.

Recently, however, the sheer size of the debt is causing even economic theorists to take it seriously. It is hard to ignore a Federal debt measured in trillions of dollars and an annual Federal deficit measured in hundreds of billions of dollars. Payments on these debts take an enormous bite out of the money which the government should be spending on job creation, rebuilding the infrastructure, feeding the hungry, constructing affordable houses, giving a first class education to our young people and training the current work force for the jobs of the future. As money disappears in interest payments on the national debt, causing worthwhile — and *necessary* — projects to be postponed for lack of funds, people are asking if there isn't a better way to finance government.

Asking the right questions about the Fed

In the center of the crisis over the government's debt problem, stands the Federal Reserve System. This powerful institution is veiled in mystery and mystique. The public is uninformed, poorly informed, or misinformed about the Fed's role in the economic scene. Our representatives, senators and other elected officials enter government service with little, if any, knowledge about how the mechanics of the Fed's money-creating system contributes to, and in fact *causes*, the nation's debt problem. How many know that:

- the twelve Federal Reserve Banks are private institutions?
- the Federal Reserve Banks create money out of nothing by writing good, unbounceable checks against no funds?
- the Federal Reserve Banks destroy the money they receive when they sell Treasury securities?
- the Fed's annual "pay-back" to the Treasury is only one half of one percent of the total Federal debt?

Has any of us ever heard a government official point out that while the debt of the U.S. Treasury is measured in *trillions* of dollars, the debt of the Federal Reserve Banks is *ZERO*? Why aren't we asking: "What is it that the Fed knows, that the Treasury doesn't?"

The debt of the 1990s: predicted in 1790

The history of the founding of the Federal Reserve System is documented in hundreds of textbooks and publications from the Fed itself. What is not so widely published is how the Fed's *money system* works. Knowledge of how this system works enables anyone to predict how big the Federal debt is going to be in the future.

For instance, Dr. Robert Blain, a professor of sociology at Southern Illinois University at Edwardsville, recently documented the fact that the multi-trillion dollar Federal debt of the 1990s was foreseen by a Georgia Congressman over 200 years ago. In an article entitled *The U.S. Debt Problem*, Dr. Blain writes:

On February 9, 1790, Georgia Congressman James Jackson, speaking in the House of Representatives of the First Congress of the United States, predicted that debt would increase exponentially. Jackson was speaking against Alexander Hamilton's plan to use a funded debt to increase the money supply of the new Nation.

"Gentlemen may come forward, perhaps, and tell me, that funding the public debt will increase the circulating medium of the country, by means of its transferable quality; but this is denied by the best informed men. The funding of the debt will occasion enormous taxes for the payment of interest. These taxes will bear heavily, both on agriculture and commerce. It will be charging the active and industrious citizen...to pay the indolent and idle creditor. In the proportion that it benefits the one, it will depress the other....

"I contend that a funding system in this country will be highly dangerous to the welfare of the Republic; it may, for a moment, raise our credit, and increase our circulation by multiplying a new species of currency; but it must hereafter settle upon our posterity a burden which they can neither bear nor relieve themselves from. It will establish a precedent in America that may, and in all probability will, be pursued by the sovereign authority, until it brings upon us that ruin which it has never failed to bring. Let us take warning by the errors of Europe, and guard against the introduction of a system followed by calamities so general. Though our present debt be but a few million, in the course of a single century it may be

multiplied to an extent we dare not think of." (Annals of Congress, Vol. I, February 1790:1141-1142)

How was Rep. Jackson able to predict the future so accurately? He had no knowledge of the prosperity which was to come to the new nation...or the wars that were to be fought...or the institutions that would administer the money system...or the people who might be in charge of these institutions.

The reason is that Rep. Jackson understood the *mechanics* of the debt-money system. He knew that allowing the banks to create money as debt and lend this money to the government at interest would eventually lead to a ruinous Federal debt, periods of inflation, depression and, ultimately, a general decline in living standards.

What James Jackson knew...that today's Congressmen don't

Rep. James Jackson learned how the debt-money system works from studying history. Today — over 200 years after his prophetic words were spoken — a smoke screen seems to hide the inner workings of the money system, making it difficult to understand its mechanisms and mathematics.

In 1980, however, the view became clearer. In that year the first edition of *The Truth In Money Book* was published. *The Truth In Money Book* explains the mechanics of the debt-money system in straightforward language. This book uncovers what is wrong with the system and tells how to fix it. *The Truth In Money Book* then describes a money system that is mathematically balanced, infla-tion-proof and depression-proof.

Figuring out the Fed gives a quick overview of the most important elements of the debt-money system. It also outlines the way a balanced U.S. Treasury money system can operate. The questions it answers are the ones which come up most frequently in discussions about the Federal Reserve. The supporting references are in the public domain and available from Federal Reserve or Government Printing Office publications.

Misplaced ridicule

Ridiculing public officials is a common pastime. While government is a long way from perfection, nothing could be more damaging to the future of democratic institutions than the constant criticizing and trivializing of elected officials and the offices they hold. A large measure of the criticism heaped on these officials because of economic conditions is actually misplaced. It is the officers of the Federal Reserve System, and not elected officials, who carry out monetary policy. As you will see as you read this book, publicly elected officials are *barred* from attending meetings where decisions affecting the economy are made. Along the same lines, the claim that the government "runs a printing press" to pay for its expenses is a lie. You need to refer to *The Truth In Money Book* for the full story.

The government debt problem has been allowed to continue this long and reach such serious proportions simply because there has been a lack of basic information about the mechanics of the money system. *The Truth In Money Book* and *Figuring out the Fed* were written to meet this need.

Margaret Thoren
Chagrin Falls, Ohio

Table of Contents

Figuring out the Fed

Frequently asked questions about the Fed

Is the Federal Reserve money system run by the President of the United States? The Secretary of the Treasury? The Congress?

No. No. No.

 Congress created the Federal Reserve back in 1913 but Congress doesn't run it. Neither does the President of the United States.

(*The Hats the Federal Reserve Wears*, Federal Reserve Bank of Philadelphia, page 13.)

Who *does* run the Federal Reserve System?

The twelve Regional Federal Reserve Banks and the commercial banks.

 The System is composed of a central Board of Governors located in Washington, D.C., and twelve regional Reserve Banks serving geographic districts. District Bank presidents work with the Board of Governors to determine central bank policy.

(*Your Money and the Federal Reserve System*, Federal Reserve Bank of Minneapolis, page 7.)

3 Is the Board of Governors of the Federal Reserve in Washington, D.C. all there is to the Federal Reserve System?

No.

Board of Governors

Regional Reserve Banks

Commercial Banks and Thrift Institutions

American Public

(*Keeping our Money Healthy*, Federal Reserve Bank of New York, page 9.)

4 What groups constitute the Federal Reserve System?

- The Board of Governors, which is called a government agency, although it has never received any government appropriations nor is it subservient to the will of Congress.
- The 12 regional Federal Reserve Banks located in Boston, New York, Philadelphia, Cleveland, Richmond, Atlanta, Chicago, St. Louis, Dallas, Kansas City, Minneapolis and San Francisco.
- The thousands of commercial banks throughout the country.

> **"** The System has several important parts:
> member banks, the Federal Reserve Banks, the
> Board of Governors, the Federal Open Market
> Committee, and the Federal Advisory
> Council...At the base of the Federal Reserve
> pyramid are the System's member banks. **"**
>
> (*The Federal Reserve at Work*, Federal Reserve Bank
> of Richmond, page 3.)

Does the United States Treasury own any stock in the
Federal Reserve Banks?

No.

Does the Congress of the United States own any stock in
the Federal Reserve Banks?

No.

Do privately-owned commercial banks own the stock of
the Federal Reserve Banks?

Yes.

Are the employees of the Federal Reserve Banks under
Civil Service?

No.

> When the Federal Reserve was created, its stock was sold to the member banks. As stockholders, they elect some of the directors of the 12 Federal Reserve Banks. The other directors are appointed by the Board of Governors. The directors and the officers they select run the Federal Reserve Banks and their 20,000 or more employees, who are not under Civil Service.

(*The Hats the Federal Reserve Wears*, Federal Reserve Bank of Philadelphia, page 14.)

Are the Federal Reserve Banks listed with government agencies in the telephone directories of the 12 cities in which they are located?

No.

87	BUSINESS-PROFESSIONAL-ORGANIZATIONAL

FEDERAL EXPRESS
Package Pick-Up & Information ------ 361-0872
Drop-Off Locations-
5339 Canal Rd ------------------ 361-0872
Cleveland-Hopkins International
Airport--------------------- 361-0872
1815 E 12 St-------------------- 361-0872
Federal Express Corp 5339 Canal Rd-- 361-0872
Federal Flavors Inc 3116 Berea Rd --- 671-6300
FEDERAL GEAR INC
1754 E 47 St ------------------ 361-4940

Federal Government Services
Such As
INTERNAL REVENUE
SOCIAL SECURITY
VETERANS ADMINISTRATION
POST OFFICES-MILITARY ETC
See GOVERNMENT OFFICES
IN THE BLUE PAGES

Federal Home Life Ins-
Harold P Hatridge Life Manager
7123 Pearl Rd----------------- 842-6500
Federal Home Life Ins Co
20525 Center Ridge Rd ---------- 331-3661
Federal Home Loan Bank
629 Euclid Av ----------------- 589-9490

FEDERAL PRODUCTS CORP
7547 Mentor Rd Mentor Ohio ------ 946-9222
FEDERAL RESERVE BANK OF CLEVE-
E 6 St & Superior Av -------------- 579-2000
Supervision Of Banks
E 6 St & Superior Av ----------- 579-2190
Money Market Deposit Rate
Information E 6 St & Superior Av -- 579-2001
Employment Information
E 6 St & Superior Av ----------- 579-2137
Public Information
E 6 St & Superior Av ----------- 579-2048
Check Collection Department-
Weekdays-5:00PM To 8:00AM
Weekends-All Day ----------- 579-2004
Savings Bonds-
Information------------------- 579-2312
Forms & Supplies-------------- 579-2287
Consignment Accounts ---------- 579-2277
Treasury Tax & Loan Accounts ----- 579-2283
Treasury Securities & Announced
Offerings E 6 St & Superior Av ---- 579-2002
Treasury Securities General
Information E 6 St & Superior Av -- 579-2490
MidAmerica Automated Payments
System MAPS E 6 St & Superior Av 579-2130
Federal Reserve Protection
Department E 6 St & Superior Av -- 579-2829
Federal Reserve Respond Park Bg --- 241-7224
FEDERAL SECURITY INC 6500 Pearl Rd ----------- **842-6562**
Federal Steel Erectors Inc
888 E 70 St ------------------- 881-7775

Excerpt from Cleveland Telephone Directory

10 Do Federal Reserve Banks pay Federal tax or State property tax?

No.

11 Do Federal Reserve Banks pay municipal property taxes?

Yes.

 3. Exemption from taxation

Federal reserve banks, including the capital stock and surplus therein, and the income derived therefrom shall be exempt from Federal, State, and local taxation, except taxes upon real estate.

(Federal Reserve Act, Board of Governors of the Federal Reserve, Section 7, Clause 3.)

Item[1]	Total
CURRENT INCOME	
Loans	25,571,333
U.S. Treasury and federal agency securities	19,262,265,500
Foreign currencies	2,499,370,712
Priced services	737,454,292
Other	28,339,977
Total	**22,553,001,814**
CURRENT EXPENSES	
Salaries and other personnel expenses	738,153,925
Retirement and other benefits[2]	101,544,004
Fees	20,456,306
Travel	32,816,521
Software expenses	32,733,641
Postage and other shipping costs	88,175,111
Communications	9,773,482
Materials and supplies	54,576,433
Building expenses	
Taxes on real estate	26,526,902

(78th Annual Report 1991, Board of Governors of the Federal Reserve, table 6, p. 254.)

12 Are the 12 regional Federal Reserve Bank privately owned corporations?

Yes.

> " The 12 regional Reserve Banks aren't government institutions but corporations nominally 'owned' by member commercial banks, who must buy special, non-marketable stock in their district Federal Reserve Bank. "
>
> (*I bet you thought...*, Federal Reserve Bank of New York, page 21.)

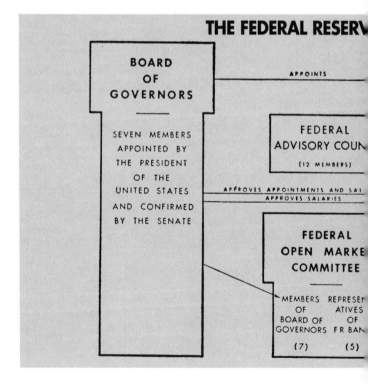

THE FEDERAL RESERV

BOARD OF GOVERNORS

APPOINTS

SEVEN MEMBERS APPOINTED BY THE PRESIDENT OF THE UNITED STATES AND CONFIRMED BY THE SENATE

FEDERAL ADVISORY COUN

(12 MEMBERS)

APPROVES APPOINTMENTS AND SAL
APPROVES SALARIES

FEDERAL OPEN MARKE COMMITTEE

MEMBERS REPRESEN
OF   ATIVES
BOARD OF   OF
GOVERNORS F R BAN
(7)   (5)

Does this mean that America's monetary policy is administered by a network of private banks?

Yes.

Does this mean that America's commercial banks are regulated by institutions *owned* by these same commercial banks?

Yes.

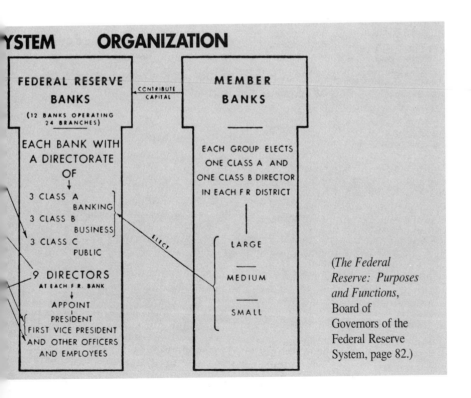

YSTEM   ORGANIZATION

FEDERAL RESERVE BANKS
(12 BANKS OPERATING 24 BRANCHES)

←CCNTRIBUTE CAPITAL→

MEMBER BANKS

EACH BANK WITH A DIRECTORATE OF
↓
3 CLASS A   BANKING
3 CLASS B   BUSINESS
3 CLASS C   PUBLIC

9 DIRECTORS
AT EACH F R. BANK
↓
APPOINT
PRESIDENT
FIRST VICE PRESIDENT
AND OTHER OFFICERS
AND EMPLOYEES

EACH GROUP ELECTS ONE CLASS A AND ONE CLASS B DIRECTOR IN EACH F R DISTRICT

ELECT

LARGE

MEDIUM

SMALL

(*The Federal Reserve: Purposes and Functions*, Board of Governors of the Federal Reserve System, page 82.)

Do the President and the Secretary of the Treasury attend the regular meetings of the Board of Governors of the Federal Reserve System where important monetary policy decisions are being made?

No.

Do members of Congress attend Board of Governors' meetings when monetary policy issues are being discussed?

No.

Are important monetary policy meetings of the Federal Reserve open to the public?...to members of Congress?...to the President of the United States?...to the Secretary of the Treasury?

No. No. No. No.

 Decisions with regard to open market operations are made by the twelve-member Federal Open Market Committee, or FOMC. This committee, which meets in Washington about eight times a year, consists of seven of the members of the Board of Governors, the President of the Federal Reserve Bank of New York, and the President of four other Reserve Banks who serve in rotation.

With regard to discount policy, the Boards of Directors of the Reserve Banks make recommendations as to changes in the discount

> rate. However, the final approval rests with the Board of Governors. Additionally, the Board of Governors has sole authority with regard to reserve requirements. **"**
>
> (*Money in the Economy*, Federal Reserve Bank of San Francisco, page 10.)

When are the reports of Federal Open Market Committee actions made public?

Important FOMC policy actions are made public a few days after the *next* meeting.

> **"** ...the "Record of Policy Actions"...is released to the public shortly after the *next* meeting of the Committee. In this way, the public is never informed of the directive currently in effect. **"**
>
> (*A Primer on the Fed*, Federal Reserve Bank of Richmond, page 52.)

Is the President of the United States a member of this important committee?

No.

Is the Secretary of the Treasury a member of this committee? Are any members of Congress on this committee? Are *any* elected officials on this committee? Are any allowed to be present when decisions are being made?

No. No. No. No.

" The Federal Open Market Committee,
composed of seven Board members and five of
the 12 Reserve Bank presidents, directs open
market operations. The Federal Open Market
Committee, or FOMC as it is known, meets
once each month in Washington. FOMC
meetings provide the focal point for Federal
Reserve assessment of the economy's
performance and decisions on what open
market policy should be. There is often
discussion as well of the use of reserve
requirements and the discount rate, although
the FOMC has no responsibility for these tools. **"**

(*Open Market Operations*, Federal Reserve Bank of
New York, page 13.)

" The Federal Open Market Committee (FOMC)
is the most important monetary policy-making
body of the Federal Reserve System. It is
responsible for the formulation of a policy
designed to promote economic growth, full
employment, stable prices, and a balance in
international trade and payments. The FOMC
makes key decisions regarding the conduct of
open market operations — purchases and sales
of U.S. Government and other securities —
which affect the provision of reserves to the
banking system and, in turn, the cost and
availability of credit in the U.S. economy.

By statute, the committee determines its own
organization. At its first meeting on or after

March 1st of each year, the committee elects staff officers to serve the committee for the coming year. Traditionally, the Chairman of the Board of Governors is elected as chairman and the President of the Federal Reserve Bank of New York as vice chairman. Staff officers are selected from among the officers and employees of the Board of Governors and the Federal Reserve Banks. Officers include: a secretary to maintain a record of actions taken by the committee upon all questions of policy; economists to prepare and present to the committee information regarding business and credit conditions and domestic and international economic and financial developments; general counsel to furnish such legal advice as the committee may require; and a manager and deputy managers of the System Open Market Account to execute open market transactions and to report to the committee on market conditions.

The law requires that meetings of the FOMC be held at least four times each year in Washington, D.C. upon the call of the Chairman of the Board of Governors or at the request of any three members of the committee. Typically, meetings are held once every 4 to 6 weeks in the offices of the Board of Governors in Washington, according to a schedule tentatively agreed upon at the beginning of the year. If circumstances require consultation or consideration of an action

Continued...

between these regular meetings, members may be called on to participate in a special meeting or a telephone conference, or to vote on a recommended action by telegram or telephone. At each regular meeting, the committee votes on the policy to be carried out during the interval between meetings; at least twice a year the committee also votes on certain longer-run policy objectives.

Attendance at meetings is restricted because of the confidential nature of financial information discussed, and is limited to committee members, nonmember Reserve Bank Presidents, staff officers, the manager and deputy managers of the system account, and a small number of Board and Reserve Bank staff. **99**

(*The Federal Open Market Committee*, Board of Governors of the Federal Reserve System, page 2.)

What are Open Market Operations?

They are the purchases and sales of government securities, and other securities, carried out by the Federal Reserve.

Where do these operation take place?

At the trading desk of the Federal Reserve Bank of New York.

> After the Federal Open Market Committee (FOMC) determines the appropriate direction of policy, the Federal Reserve Bank of New York (acting on behalf of the system) purchases U.S. Government or government-agency securities in the open market from major securities dealers. It pays with checks drawn on itself, thus generating newly-created deposits with the Federal Reserve.
>
> (*Money in the Economy*, Federal Reserve Bank of San Francisco, page 6.)

23 Where does the Federal Reserve Bank of New York get the money to buy the government bonds?

The Federal Reserve Bank of New York *creates* the money that it uses to buy the government bonds.

> Now, the reason that the Federal Reserve can increase the money supply by buying government securities on the open market and decrease the money supply by selling government securities is because the Federal Reserve has a unique responsibility — it can literally create its own credit. Let me use an everyday example to make the point. If I were to buy a government bond from one of you, what that would mean is that I would give you a check for, say, $10,000, and you would in return give me that government bond worth
>
> *Continued...*

$10,000. What left my checking account when I bought the bond entered your checking account when you sold it. The total volume of checking account money in the economy has not changed one penny. What has happened is a simple transfer of some of that money from one account to another. Put another way, I cannot, legally or morally, write a check payable to you unless I have at least that much in my checking account at the time I write the check.

The Federal Reserve is different. It is the central bank; it is a depository for all of the member banks, but it, itself, has no bank deposit anywhere in the country because it is the central bank of the entire country. When you or I write a check there must be sufficient funds in our account to cover that check, but when the Federal Reserve writes a check, it is creating money. That check, written by the Federal Reserve, is deposited in the account of one commercial bank, but is not deducted from the account of another commercial bank. 99

(*Putting it simply...*, Federal Reserve Bank of Boston, page 17.)

24 Where do the Federal Reserve banks get the money they use to pay for their general expenses?

They create it out of nothing, just as they create money out of nothing to pay for government securities.

> Earlier sections of this booklet described the way in which bank reserves increase when the Federal Reserve purchases securities and decline when the Fed sells securities. The same results follow from any Federal Reserve expenditure or receipt. Every payment made by the Reserve banks, in meeting expenses or acquiring any assets, affect bank deposits and reserves in the same way as does the payment to a dealer for government securities. Similarly, Reserve bank receipts of interest on loans and securities and increases in paid-in capital absorb reserves. **"**
>
> (*Modern Money Mechanics*, Federal Reserve Bank of Chicago, page 28.)

Does the Congress determine or regulate the amount of money which the Federal Reserve System creates? What about the President of the United States or the Secretary of the Treasury — do they determine how much money there is in the economy?

No. No.

> We begin by explaining what economists mean when they talk about 'money', and how banks and other depository institutions can 'create' money. We then explain how monetary policy is made in the United States and describe the policy instruments the Federal Reserve System
>
> *Continued...*

has at its disposal to control the size of the
money supply — the total amount of money
circulating in the national economy. This leads
us to a discussion of how Federal Reserve
actions in making the money supply grow
faster or slower affect important economic
magnitudes like interest rates, unemployment,
and inflation. Finally we describe the
operating procedure used by the Federal
Reserve to carry out monetary policy.

(*Money in the Economy*, Federal Reserve Bank of San
Francisco, page 3.)

26 Does the Federal Reserve ever take steps to decrease
the money supply?

Yes.

 Now suppose some reduction in the volume of
money is desired... Just as purchases of
government securities by the Federal Reserve
System can provide the basis for deposit
expansion by adding to bank reserves, sales of
securities by the Federal Reserve System
reduce the money stock by absorbing bank
reserves.

(*Modern Money Mechanics*, Federal Reserve Bank of
Chicago, page 12.)

27 How does the Federal Reserve cause the money supply to decline?

The Federal Reserve Banks sell some of the government securities they hold. The buyer gives the Fed a check for the securities and the Fed simply destroys this money and wipes it out of the money supply.

 When the Federal Reserve sells securities, the supply of lendable money is decreased.

...when the Federal Reserve sells a government security, the check paying for it is deducted from the account of the commercial bank on which it is drawn, but it is not deposited to the account of another commercial bank.

(*Putting it simply*..., Federal Reserve Bank of Boston, pages 16, 17.)

28 What happens to the economy when the money supply decreases?

People are unable to get hold of the money they need to pay their debts and eventually bankruptcies increase, business activity slows down, unemployment increases and a recession or depression takes place.

(*The Story of Banks*, Federal Reserve Bank of New York, page 7.)

29 What specific clause in the Federal Reserve Act of 1913 (the Act which established the Federal Reserve System) gives the Federal Reserve Banks the authority to create and destroy money?

There isn't one.

30 Do the Federal Reserve Banks use gold to create money?

No. The Federal Reserve Banks create money out of nothing. The money they create enters the economy in the form of checks which each bank draws "on itself."

> ❝ Put another way, when the Federal Reserve buys government securities, it is by the mere stroke of a pen putting new money into the banking system — money which itself can lead to the creation of even more new money.
>
> When the Federal Reserve writes a check, it is creating money. ❞
>
> (*Putting it simply...*, Federal Reserve Bank of Boston, page 17.)

31 When the Federal Reserve Banks destroy or extinguish parts of the money supply, where does this money go?

It goes back to nothing.

> ❝ Just as purchases of government securities by the Federal Reserve System can provide the basis for deposit expansion by adding to bank reserves, sales of securities by the Federal Reserve System reduce the money stock by absorbing bank reserves. The process is essentially the reverse of the expansion steps just described. ❞
>
> (*Modern Money Mechanics*, Federal Reserve Bank of Chicago, page 12.)

32 What government agency operates the Bureau of Engraving and Printing?

The United States Treasury.

How does the Treasury receive orders to print Federal Reserve Bank notes?

The Treasury receives its orders to print Federal Reserve notes from the 12 regional Federal Reserve Banks. The 12 regional Federal Reserve Banks simply collect orders for notes from the commercial banks in their respective districts and pass these along to the Bureau of Engraving and Printing in Washington.

Does the Federal government "run the printing press" to pay for its expenses?

No.

 The Bureau of Engraving and Printing in Washington, D.C., a unit of the Treasury, is responsible for printing the nation's currency. But its orders to print come from the 12 Federal Reserve Banks, not the President or Congress. The Reserve Banks, not the Treasury, determine how much currency is printed, based mainly on estimates of commercial bank and public cash demands. Under this arrangement, the government can't print more Federal Reserve notes to pay its bills or debts.

Since most U.S. money is checkbook money, the printing presses have little to do with the buying power of money. **99**

(*I bet you thought...*, Federal Reserve Bank of New York, page 12.)

If the government "ran the printing press" to pay its expenses, could it ever be in debt?

No.

Even though the Bureau of Engraving and Printing presses in Washington are run by the Treasury, couldn't we say that it is actually the Federal Reserve System which "runs the printing press" in the United States?

Yes.

What is the debt of the Federal Reserve Banks?

The debt of the twelve Federal Reserve Banks is ZERO.

The Federal Reserve Banks do not borrow; neither does the Board of Governors. The 12 regional Federal Reserve Banks and the Board of Governors have never received any government appropriations. Nor has either been subjected to a full Government Accounting Office audit.

1. Detailed Statement of Condition of All Federal Reserve Banks Combined, December 31, 1991 [1]

Thousands of dollars

ASSETS

Gold certificate account			11,058,778
Special drawing rights certificate account			10,018,000
Coin			527,613

Loans and securities

Loans to depository institutions		218,356	
Federal agency obligations			
Bought outright		6,044,500	
Held under repurchase agreement		552,850	
U.S. Treasury securities			
Bought outright			
Bills	132,635,005		
Notes	101,519,719		
Bonds	32,331,474		
Total bought outright		266,486,198	
Held under repurchase agreement		15,345,150	
Total securities		281,831,348	
Total loans and securities			288,647,054

Items in process of collection

Transit items		7,093,797	
Other items in process of collection		1,191,655	
Total items in process of collection			8,285,452

Bank premises

Land		144,591	
Buildings (including vaults)	690,804		
Building machinery and equipment	191,695		
Construction account	199,872		
Total bank premises		1,082,371	
Less depreciation allowance		240,249	842,122
Bank premises, net			986,714

Other assets

Furniture and equipment		819,345	
Less depreciation		480,008	
Total furniture and equipment, net		339,337	
Denominated in foreign currencies [2]		27,626,276	
Interest accrued		3,111,150	
Premium on securities		1,869,578	
Overdrafts		17,312	
Prepaid expenses		354,413	
Suspense account		12,698	
Real estate acquired for banking-house purposes		16,753	
Other		189,675	
Total other assets			33,537,192
Total assets			**353,060,803**

LIABILITIES

Federal Reserve Notes

Outstanding (issued to Federal Reserve Banks)		366,467,574	
Less held by Federal Reserve Banks		78,561,962	
Total Federal Reserve notes, net			287,905,612

Deposits

Depository institutions			29,412,997
U.S. Treasury, general account			17,696,902
Foreign, official accounts			967,609

Other deposits

Officers' and certified checks		19,932	
International organizations		79,778	
Other [3]		1,606,070	
Total other deposits			1,705,780
Deferred credit items			7,259,372

Other liabilities		
Discount on securities	2,319,224	
Sundry items payable	72,311	
Suspense account	34,095	
All other	383,884	
Total other liabilities		**2,809,514**
Total liabilities		**347,757,787**
CAPITAL ACCOUNTS		
Capital paid in		**2,651,508**
Surplus		**2,651,508**
Other capital accounts [4]		**0**
Total liabilities and capital accounts		**353,060,803**

1. Amounts in boldface type indicate items in the Board's weekly statement of condition of the Federal Reserve Banks.
2. Of this amount $8,152.3 million was invested in securities issued by foreign governments, and the balance was invested with foreign central banks and the Bank for International Settlements.

3. In closing out the other capital accounts at year-end, the Reserve Bank earnings that are payable to the Treasury are included in this account pending payment.
4. During the year, includes undistributed net income, which is closed out on Dec. 31.

(*78th Annual Report 1991*, Board of Governors of the Federal Reserve System, table 1, pages 244-245)

PUBLIC LAW 95-320—JULY 21, 1978   92 STAT. 391

Public Law 95-320
95th Congress   July 21, 1978
An Act   [H.R. 2176]

To amend the Accounting and Auditing Act of 1950 to provide for the audit, by the Comptroller General of the United States, of the Federal Reserve System.

(3)   An audit made under paragraph (1) (A) shall not include—

(A)   transactions conducted on behalf of or with foreign central banks, foreign governments, and nonprivate international financing organizations;

(B)   deliberations, decisions, and actions on monetary policy matters, including discount window operations, reserves of member banks, securities credit, interest on deposits, and open market operations;

(C)   transactions made under the direction of the Federal Open Market Committee including transactions of the Federal Reserve System Open Market Account; and

(D)   those portions of oral, written, telegraphic, or telephonic discussions and communications among or between Members of Board of Governors, and officers and employees of the Federal Reserve System which deal with topics listed in subparagraphs (A), (B), and (C) of this paragraph.

38 Doesn't the fact that the Federal Reserve Banks have *no* debt prove what a tremendous advantage it is to be able to create money and lend or spend it into circulation?

Yes.

39 According to the United States Constitution, what branch of the Federal government has the authority to create money and regulate its value?

The Congress.

 Section 8. The Congress shall have Power...To coin Money, regulate the Value thereof, and of foreign Coin, and fix the Standard of Weights and Measures:...

(U.S. Constitution, Article 1, Section 8, Clause 5.)

40 Has the Federal Reserve System assumed the Congressional authority to create money?

Yes.

41 But does the Constitutional prerogative to create money still rest with the Congress, despite what the Federal Reserve is doing?

Yes.

Do the 12 regional Federal Reserve Banks earn profits?

Yes.

How much income did they have in 1991?

Approximately $22.6 billion.

Where did this money come from?

Mainly from the interest the Treasury paid to the Federal Reserve on the government bonds which the Fed bought with the money it created by writing good, unbounceable checks against no funds.

6. Income and Expenses of Federal Reserve Banks, 1991 Dollars	
Item [1]	Total
CURRENT INCOME	
Loans..........................	25,571,333
U.S. Treasury and federal agency securities	19,262,265,500 ←
Foreign currencies.............	2,499,370,712
Priced services	737,454,292
Other	28,339,977
Total	22,553,001,814

(*78th Annual Report 1991*, Board of Governors of the Federal Reserve System, table 6, page 254.)

Where does the Treasury get the money it needs to pay the interest it owes to the Federal Reserve Banks?

Mainly from the taxes it collects from individuals and corporations.

Where does the Federal Reserve get the money which it uses to buy government bonds?

The Federal Reserve simply creates the money out of nothing.

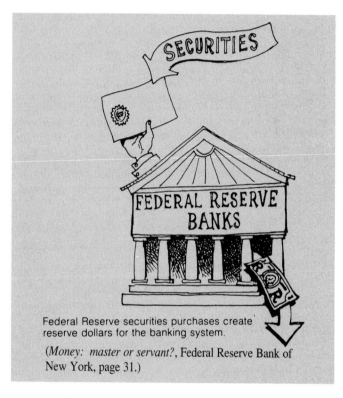

Federal Reserve securities purchases create reserve dollars for the banking system.

(*Money: master or servant?*, Federal Reserve Bank of New York, page 31.)

The Federal Reserve records that its expenses were $1.6 billion in 1991. So its profit was around $21 billion. What did the Federal Reserve do with this profit that it earned in 1991?

The Fed paid the money back to the Treasury. This payment has been called the "Franchise Tax" and also "The payment under section 13b." Today it is known as "Interest on Federal Reserve Notes." But there's more. See Question #51.

Table 7

Dividends paid to Regional Federal Reserve Banks	Interest on Federal Reserve Notes
1987 — 117,499,115	17,738,879,542
1988 — 125,616,018	17,364,318,571
1989 — 129,885,339	21,646,417,306
1990 — 140,757,879	23,608,397,730
1991 — 152,553,160	20,777,552,290

(*78th Annual Report 1991*, Board of Governors of the Federal Reserve System, table 7, page 261.)

Is it any sacrifice for the Federal Reserve to pay back this amount of money to the Treasury?

No, because the Federal Reserve can always *create* as much money as it wants to buy government bonds, to meet its expenses, or to buy any kind of asset.

What is the national debt in 1993?

$4,463,400,000,000 - $4.5 trillion.

50 What percentage of the national debt was the 1991 Federal Reserve payback?

It is about one-half of one percent (0.005%).

51 Did the Federal Reserve payback reduce the Federal debt?

Only by a tiny — actually negligible — amount. $21 billion is peanuts next to the trillions of dollars of debt which the debt-money system has generated. Even the total amount paid to the Treasury since the Fed was founded in 1913 is only $281 billion — which is six percent of the total national debt. In return, the debt-money system administered by the Fed for the past eighty years has put the country in debt to the tune of trillions of dollars.

7. Income and Expenses of Federal Reserve Banks, 1914-91 Dollars

Payments to U.S. Treasury			
	Franchise tax	Under section 13b	Interest on Federal Reserve notes
Total, 1914-91	$149,138,300	$2,188,893	$281,009,629,148

(78th Annual Report 1991, Board of Governors of the Federal Reserve system, table 7, pages 260-261.)

52 So the payback isn't such an act of generosity as it seems?

It is no act of generosity at all when you consider the

fact that the Federal Reserve's money system *causes* the multi-trillion debt in the first place.

How much money will the Internal Revenue Service collect from individuals in 1993?

Approximately $507 billion.

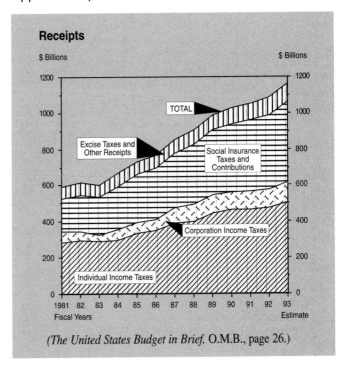

(The United States Budget in Brief, O.M.B., page 26.)

How much of this $507 billion will be used to pay *interest* on the national debt?

$210.3 billion which is 41%.

55 So, 41% of the taxes paid by individuals goes just to pay interest on what the government has borrowed?

Yes.

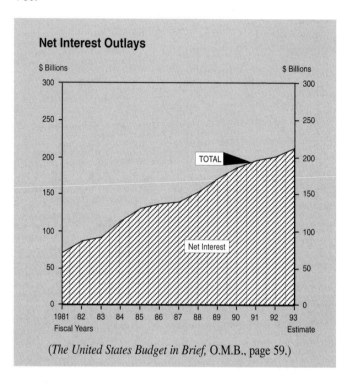

Net Interest Outlays

$ Billions .... $ Billions

(The United States Budget in Brief, O.M.B., page 59.)

56 Could the government operate *without* debt if it used its Constitutional prerogative to create money?

Yes. (See *The Truth In Money Book,* pages 158, 202-203.)

57 Are the privately owned Federal Reserve Banks using the government's Constitutional money-creating powers to create money to lend *to the Federal Government at interest?*

Yes.

Is the Federal Reserve System's money-creating method contributing to the government's growing debt?

Yes. The flaws in the system constitute the fundamental cause of the national debt.

What is the debt of the Federal government?

$4.5 trillion.

What is the total debt of the Federal Reserve Banks?

ZERO.

So, if the Congress started using its Constitutional power to create money, the government could operate without debt, just as the Federal Reserve Banks do today?

Yes.

If the government operated without debt, could taxes be reduced?

Yes. Taxes could be slashed and ultimately the income tax could be abolished. (See *The Truth In Money Book,* pages 196, 208.)

Frequently asked questions about banking

63 Do commercial banks create money?

Yes.

COMMERCIAL BANKS, HOWEVER, LEND IN A DIFFERENT WAY. THEY CREATE NEW CHECKBOOK DOLLARS AND ADD THEM TO A BORROWER'S CHECKING ACCOUNT. BECAUSE COMMERCIAL BANKS CREATE ALMOST ALL NEW DOLLARS, THEY PLAY A SPECIAL ROLE IN OUR FINANCIAL SYSTEM.

LOANS

(*The Story of Banks*, Federal Reserve Bank of New York, page 4.)

64 What about thrift institutions (credit unions, mutual savings banks, savings and loans)? Do they create the money they lend?

Until the 1980s, the thrift institutions were "middle men" — taking in savings and lending the money primarily for home building loans and mortgages.

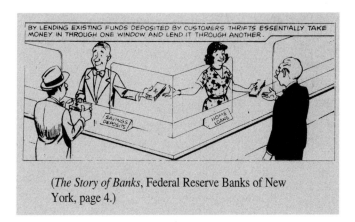

BY LENDING EXISTING FUNDS DEPOSITED BY CUSTOMERS THRIFTS ESSENTIALLY TAKE MONEY IN THROUGH ONE WINDOW AND LEND IT THROUGH ANOTHER.

SAVINGS DEPOSITS

HOME LOANS

(*The Story of Banks*, Federal Reserve Banks of New York, page 4.)

65 What happened in the 1980s?

Congress passed two Acts — one in 1980 and another in 1982. The effect of these Acts was to enable some thrifts to make commercial loans; in other words, to create money.

 The Depository Institutions Deregulation and Monetary Control Act of 1980 permitted S&Ls to make various types of consumer loans and to provide consumer transactions accounts, thus allowing S&Ls to compete head-to-head with banks for virtually the entire range of household business.

The Garn-St. Germain Act of 1982 further expanded S&Ls' asset and liability powers, particularly in the commercial area.

(*Economic Commentary*, December 1, 1988, Federal Reserve Bank of Cleveland.)

66 Did the change from "money middle men" to money creators contribute to the savings and loan crisis?

Yes.

> **66** ...in the Act (1982), S&Ls were authorized to make any type of commercial loan (including unsecured ones) and to offer demand deposit services to their commercial customers. Thus, the Act allowed S&Ls to enter a product market that, due to regulation, had largely been the private preserve of commercial banks.
>
> Entry into nontraditional activities like commercial lending could either strengthen or weaken thrifts.
>
> ...start-up costs could be high and inexperience could result in unintentional, excessive risk-taking and subsequent losses. S&Ls' entry and aggressive competition for incremental business could cause lending margins to shrink or vanish. Further, these additional powers were authorized at a time when S&Ls' earnings were generally weak or nonexistent and their capital levels were low and eroding. Thus, even a few lending decisions that proved to be wrong could be fatal. **99**
>
> (*Economic Commentary*, December 1, 1988, Federal Reserve Bank of Cleveland.)

67 How much will the savings and loan bailout cost the American taxpayers?

The cost to the taxpayers stood at $85 billion (as of the end of 1992) and is estimated to go as high as $200 billion. A newspaper article noted that the bailout will exceed the *combined* U.S. resources devoted to Europe under the Marshall Plan, *plus* the bailouts of Lockheed, Chrysler, Penn Central and New York City.

Do commercial banks create the money that they lend?

Yes.

(*The Story of Money*, Federal Reserve Bank of New York, page 4.)

Is the "prime rate" the lowest rate at which commercial banks lend to their most credit-worthy customers?

No.

Is the "prime rate" set by the President of the United Sates?...the Secretary of the Treasury?...the Congress?

No. No. No.

Does the Board of Governors of the Federal Reserve System set the "prime rate"?

No.

Do the large New York City banks set the "prime rate"?

Yes.

*The Washington Post on the same date reported:
'The prime rate is the interest banks charge their most creditworthy corporate customers.'*

And so it went in newspapers across the nation and on the evening network news shows.

The American public, including prospective borrowers, had every reason to believe that, indeed, the lowest possible interest rate that could be expected on a commercial loan at U.S. banks was 17 percent on May 8, 1980.

Months later — on July 17, 1980 — the Federal Reserve Board cast serious doubt on these news reports and assumptions, replying to a request from the Banking, Finance and Urban Affairs Committee with a survey which showed that 60.7 percent of commercial loans granted by large commercial banks in New

York during May of 1980 were below the publicly announced prime rate.[1] In fact, the Federal Reserve reported to the Committee that at these large New York City banks, the average discount from the prime rate was 4.26 percentage points.

In May of 1980, was the prime rate 17 percent as announced by the commercial banking industry, or was it less than 13 percent as determined by the average commercial rate revealed in the Federal Reserve study?

---

1.   The phrase "prime rate" took on a formal meaning in 1933 when the industry adopted a 1 1/2 percent rate for its most preferred customers, a move prompted, in part, by efforts to stabilize the industry and to dampen what some felt could be excessive efforts to compete for the limited number of truly "prime" customers remaining in the economy. Prior to 1933, many banks did post "prime rates" but these were not publicized and tended to vary across the nation.

For seventeen years, the prime remained at the depression-era 1 1/2 percent. The prime continued to be an extremely stable rate through the 1950s and the first half of the 1960s. Since that time, the rate has been much more volatile with large and frequent changes. In the late 1970s and into the first part of the present decade (the 1980s), it has not been unusual for prime rate announcements to occur on a week by week basis.

Continued...

MANUFACTURERS HANOVER TRUST COMPANY

350 PARK AVENUE, NEW YORK, N. Y. 10022

JOHN R. TORELL III
VICE CHAIRMAN

March 6, 1981

Representative Fernand J. St. Germain,
Chairman
Committee on Banking, Finance and
Urban Affairs
U.S. House of Representatives
2129 Rayburn House Office Building
Washington, D.C. 20515

Dear Representative St. Germain:

I am replying to your letter of February 12, 1981 in which you
requested information concerning the Prime Rate. Manufacturers
Hanover Trust Company does have a publicly stated Prime Rate and
periodic changes are made a matter of public record at the time of
each change. A small group of senior officers which constitute
the Office of the Chairman has responsiblity for determination of
the Bank's current Prime Rate, and decisions to change the rate
are based upon an assessment of current and future loan demand,
current funding costs and other appropriate economic factors. A
substantial portion of our lending to commercial and industrial
customers is done on a basis related to our Prime Rate.

There are, however, certain types of lending which may result in
rates being offered that are less than the current Prime Rate at a
given time. Some of these lending activities may involve: 1) Our
Small Business Base Rate which is set at 1 1/4% under our current
Prime Rate and is made available to those companies with assets of
no more than $1,500,000 and whose total borrowings are not more
than $500,000. 2) Our Money Market Rate facility which is spar-
ingly used and offered generally for one day duration. It is
principally used by companies who balance their positions in the
commercial paper market. 3) Tax-exempt lending related to Industrial Development Bond facilities where the rates reflect the fact
that income from such loans is not subject to Federal income
taxes. 4) In an environment of rising interest rates such as
occurred during 1980, fixed-rate term loan facilities can occa-
sionally result in a loan being booked at a rate below Prime
although originally set at or near Prime since the rate will en-
dure throughout the extended life of the transaction. **99**

(*An Analysis of Prime Lending Practices at the Ten
Largest United States Banks*, House Banking
Committee, pages 2 and 50. See also *The Truth In
Money Book*, pages 254-255.)

73

Are independent, locally owned commercial banks
being hurt by some of the policies of the Fed and the
giant international banks?

Yes.

In what way?

One way is that as the debt-money system becomes more unstable, large international banks begin buying up independent and locally owned banks. When this happens, local control is forfeited and major decisions are no longer made at the branch level.

Can the Congress influence the large New York banks to bring down the "prime rate"?

No.

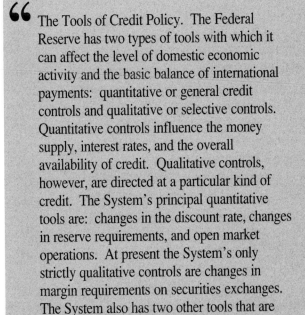

"The Tools of Credit Policy. The Federal Reserve has two types of tools with which it can affect the level of domestic economic activity and the basic balance of international payments: quantitative or general credit controls and qualitative or selective controls. Quantitative controls influence the money supply, interest rates, and the overall availability of credit. Qualitative controls, however, are directed at a particular kind of credit. The System's principal quantitative tools are: changes in the discount rate, changes in reserve requirements, and open market operations. At present the System's only strictly qualitative controls are changes in margin requirements on securities exchanges. The System also has two other tools that are partly quantitative and partly qualitative. One

Continued...

> is the setting of maximum rates payable on time and savings deposits at member banks. The other is the buying and selling of foreign currencies in the foreign exchange market. **99**
>
> (*The Federal Reserve at Work*, Federal Reserve Bank of Richmond, page 9.)

76 When the Federal Reserve and commercial banks create money as loans, do they create only the loan principal?

Yes.

77 Does this mean that the money needed to pay interest on the principal is not created when the loan is made?

Yes. The money needed to pay interest is not created within the economy.

78 Can some borrowers get their interest money from part of other people's principal?

Yes.

79 Won't this cause a shortage of money when other people try to get hold of the money they need to pay *their* principal and interest?

Yes.

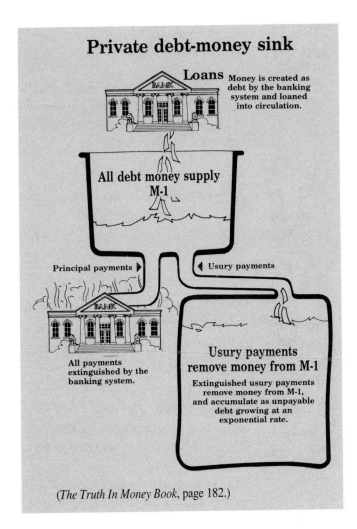

Private debt-money sink

Loans Money is created as debt by the banking system and loaned into circulation.

All debt money supply M-1

Principal payments ▶ ◀ Usury payments

All payments extinguished by the banking system.

Usury payments remove money from M-1

Extinguished usury payments remove money from M-1, and accumulate as unpayable debt growing at an exponential rate.

(The Truth In Money Book, page 182.)

80

What happens when people can't get the money they need to pay their interest?

They either go bankrupt or borrow to pay the interest.

81 Won't borrowing to pay interest cause their debts to grow faster and faster?

Yes. The debts will grow exponentially. This means that the larger the debt is, the faster it will grow. The chart for question #54 is in the form of an exponential. (See also *The Truth In Money Book* pages 86 and 134.)

82 Is this what is causing the huge growth in debt here in the United States and abroad?

Yes.

83 Does exponential debt growth cause the money system to become unstable?

Yes.

84 Does the fact that the Federal Reserve and commercial banks *lend* almost all of our money into circulation as debt contribute to the instability of the economy?

Yes. In effect, the American people are paying interest on every dollar that is in circulation.

85 Is there any way to prevent the money system from becoming more and more unstable?

Yes. Enough money must be spent into circulation debt-free to enable borrowers to repay both principal and interest without having to borrow to pay the interest.

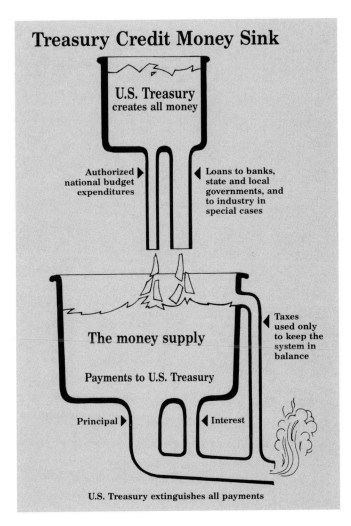

Treasury Credit Money Sink

U.S. Treasury
creates all money

Authorized ▶
national budget
expenditures

◀ Loans to banks,
state and local
governments, and
to industry in
special cases

The money supply

◀ Taxes
used only
to keep the
system in
balance

Payments to U.S. Treasury

Principal ▶   ◀ Interest

U.S. Treasury extinguishes all payments

86

Do banks extinguish the money paid to them when
borrowers repay their debts?

Yes. The money paid to commercial banks goes out of
existence and is extinguished out of the money supply.

43

> But bank credit isn't a one-way street. It adds to our money supply, to be sure, but our money supply declines as bank credit is repaid. Banks, then, can "destroy" or "extinguish" money as well as "create" it.

(*Money: master or servant?*, Federal Reserve Bank of New York, page 15. See also *The Truth In Money Book*, pages 94-96, 181, and 226.)

87 So, if money is spent into the economy debt-free, when it is used to pay principal and interest payments to commercial banks it will be removed from circulation, right?

That is correct. It is extinguished out of the money supply.

88 Is it true that because of the extinguishment process, there won't be "too much money" in the economy when debt-free money is spent into circulation?

That is correct. Repayments of money to commercial banks remove money from circulation. The debt-free money flowing in and out of the economy will have no ill effects, and will not cause inflation.

Who should spend this debt-free money into circulation?

The Treasury, under the direction of the Congress.

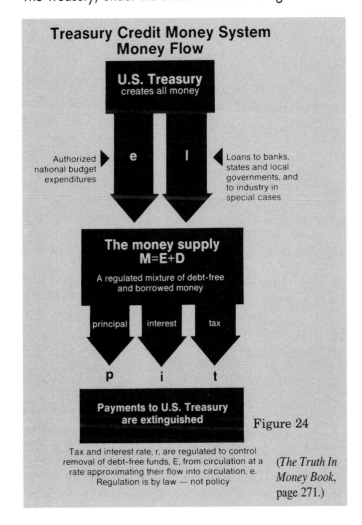

**Treasury Credit Money System
Money Flow**

U.S. Treasury
creates all money

Authorized national budget expenditures ▶ **e** | **l** ◀ Loans to banks, states and local governments, and to industry in special cases

**The money supply
M=E+D**

A regulated mixture of debt-free and borrowed money

principal | interest | tax

p | **i** | **t**

**Payments to U.S. Treasury
are extinguished**

Figure 24

Tax and interest rate, r, are regulated to control removal of debt-free funds, E, from circulation at a rate approximating their flow into circulation, e. Regulation is by law — not policy

(The Truth In Money Book, page 271.)

90 Has the Congress ever spent money into circulation?

Yes. During the Civil War, Congress instructed the Treasury to create $450 million to pay for the North's war effort. If the Treasury hadn't spent this debt-free money, we would still be paying billions of dollars of interest on the Civil War debt. The Lincoln greenbacks were anti-inflationary because they added money to the economy without adding debt to the system. Economic policy based on Treasury-issued money is called "Lincolnomics."

> ❝ *Early in 1862, the Treasury spent $60,000,000 debt-free notes into circulation. These were legal tender notes to be used to pay all debts, public and private. As they were printed with green ink on the back, they soon received their common name of 'Greenbacks'. The new money brought immediate relief to the North. Soldiers could be paid and supplies purchased without the danger of incurring debts at 24%-36% interest. The total issue of Greenbacks and the so-called 'shin plasters', which were used for small change, was $449,338,902 at its highest point.* ❞

A Greenback dated August 1, 1862
(*The Truth In Money Book*, page 143.)

91 How would a Lincolnomic money system affect banking today?

The Lincolnomic money system would benefit banking! By returning monetary authority to the Treasury, commercial banks are relieved of day-to-day liquidity brinkmanship and scrambling for reserve funds. The general prosperity of the economy would be reflected in a prosperous banking sector. (See *The Truth In Money Book*, pages 200-207.)

92 What will it take to enable the government to begin to spend money into circulation debt-free, instead of having to borrow it from the banks?

A simple Act of Congress. See *The Truth In Money Book*, pages 223-229.

93 Will spending debt-free money into circulation reduce the deficit without tax increases or painful budget cuts?

Yes. Spending debt-free money into circulation will also help to cap the national debt and eventually begin to reduce it.

94 Do we have enough Congressmen who understand the problem and the solution and who can pass the right law?

Not yet.

95 Is that why it is so important for every member of Congress to have a copy of this book?

Yes!

Index

Question
Number

References

Question Number	Reference

1   Lawrence C. Murdoch, Jr., *The Hats the Federal Reserve Wears* (Philadelphia: The Federal Reserve Bank of Philadelphia, no date given), p. 13.

2   Federal Reserve Bank of Minneapolis, *Your Money and the Federal Reserve System*, 6th ed. (Minneapolis: The Federal Reserve Bank of Minneapolis, 1982), p. 7.

3   Federal Reserve Bank of New York, *Keeping Our Money Healthy* (New York: The Federal Reserve Bank of New York, 1981), p. 9.

4   Robert P. Black, B.U. Ratchford, and A.N. Snellings, *The Federal Reserve at Work*, 6th ed. (Richmond: The Federal Reserve Bank of Richmond, 1979), p.3.

5-8   *The Hats the Federal Reserve Wears*, p. 14 (see reference 1).

9   The Cleveland Telephone Directory.

11   Board of Governors of the Federal Reserve System, *Federal Reserve Act*, 1983 ed., Section 7, Clause 3, p. 13.

        _____*78th Annual Report 1991* (Washington, D.C.: Board of Governors of the Federal Reserve System, 1991), table 6, p. 254.

12   Federal Reserve Bank of New York, *I bet you thought...* 2nd ed. (New York: The Federal Reserve Bank of New York, 1980), p. 21.

13-14   Board of Governors of the Federal Reserve System, *The Federal Reserve: Purposes and Functions* (Washington, D.C.: Board of Governors of the Federal Reserve System, 1954), p. 82.

15-17   Michael W. Keran, et. al., *Money in the Economy* (San Francisco, 1984), p. 10.

18   Alfred Broaddus, *A Primer on the Fed* (Richmond: Federal Reserve Bank of Richmond, 1988), p. 52.

19-20   Paul Meek, *Open Market Operations* (New York: The Federal Reserve Bank of New York, 1978), pp. 13-14.

Question Number	Reference
	Board of Governors of the Federal Reserve System, *The Federal Open Market Committee* (Washington, D.C.: The Board of Governors of the Federal Reserve System, 1979) p. 2.
22	*Money in the Economy*, p. 6 (see reference 15-17).
23	Federal Reserve Bank of Boston, *Putting it simply...The Federal Reserve* (Boston: The Federal Reserve Bank of Boston, 1980), p. 17.
24	Dorothy M. Nichols, *Modern Money Mechanics* (Chicago: The Federal Reserve Bank of Chicago, 1982), p. 28.
25	*Money in the Economy*, p. 3, (see reference 15-17).
26	*Modern Money Mechanics*, p. 12, (see reference 24).
27	*Putting it simply...The Federal Reserve*, p. 16, 17, (see reference 23).
28	Parnow, *The Story of Banks and Thrifts* (New York: Federal Reserve Bank of New York, 1979), p. 7.
30	*Putting it simply...The Federal Reserve*, p. 17, (see reference 23).
31	*Modern Money Mechanics*, p. 12, (see reference 24).
34	I bet you thought..., p. 12, (see reference 12).
37	*78th Annual Report 1991*, table 1, pp. 244-245, (see reference 11).
	U.S. Congress, *An act...to provide for the audit...of the Federal Reserve*, Public L 95-320, 95th Congress, 2nd Session, 1978, H.R. 2176.
39	U.S., Constitution, Article I, Section 8, Clause 5.
44	*78th Annual Report 1991*, table 6, p. 254, (see references 11).
46	Thomas O. Waage, *Money: master or servant?* (New York: Federal Reserve Bank of New York, 1980), p. 31.
47	*78th Annual Report 1991*, table 7, p. 261, (see reference 11).
49	U.S., Congress, Joint Economic Committee, *Economic Indicators* Prepared by the Council of Economic Advisers (Washington, D.C.: Government Printing Office, December, 1992), page 32.
51	*78th Annual Report 1991*, table 7, pp. 260-261, (see reference 11).

Question Number	Reference

53   Executive Office of the President, Office of Management and Budget, *The United States Budget in Brief FY 1989* (Washington, D.C.: Government Printing Office, 1988), p. 45.

Ibid., *Economic Indicators* p. 33.

54   *The United States Budget in Brief FY 1989*, p. 86.

63   *The Story of Banks* and Thrifts, p. 4, (see reference 28).

64   Ibid.

65   Whalen, Gary, "Commercial Lending of Ohio's S&Ls," *Economic Commentary* published by the Federal Reserve Bank of Cleveland, December 1, 1988.

66   Ibid.

67   Pike, Christopher J. and James B. Thomson, "The RTC and the Escalating Costs of the Thrift Insurance Mess." *Economic Commentary* published by the Federal Reserve Bank of Cleveland, May 1, 1991.

Resolution Trust Corporation public affairs office document, "TRC Scorecard", December 21, 1992.

"Plan tackles savings and loan ills." *The Christian Science Monitor*, 1 December 1988, p.3.

68   D.H. Friedman and C.J. Parnow, *The Story of Money*, (New York: Federal Reserve Bank of New York, 1984), p. 4.

72   Committee on Banking, Finance and Urban Affairs, House of Representatives, *An Analysis of Prime Lending Practices at the Ten Largest United States Banks* (Washington, D.C.: Government Printing Office, 1981), pp. 2, 50.

75   *The Federal Reserve at Work*, p. 9 (see reference 4).

79   T. R. Thoren and R. F. Warner, *The Truth In Money Book*, (Chagrin Falls: Truth In Money, Inc., 1989), p. 182.

85   Ibid., p. 187.

86   *Money: master or servant?*, p. 14 (see reference 6).

89   *The Truth In Money Book*, p. 271 (see reference 79).

90   Ibid., p. 143.

About the author

Margaret Thoren graduated from The Pennsylvania State University with a BA (Honors) in English. After teaching junior high school for one year in Washington state, she moved to London where she worked for *The Economist Newspaper* and later became editor of *The Bankers' Magazine*. After ten years in England, she returned to the United States and launched a freelance writing and editing career. She is the editor of *The Truth In Money Book*.

Photo by Jennie Campana

Order Form

Yes! I want to help solve the deficit problem! Yes! I want to help solve the problem of the $5 trillion national debt! Yes! I want to help others "figure out the Fed"!

1. Please rush me the following copies of *Figuring out the Fed:*

_____ for the President and his staff

_____ for my two Senators and their staffs

_____ for my Representative and staff

_____ for my local School Board President, Mayor and other local officials

_____ for my family and friends

1 to 5 copies:	$7.95 each post paid
6 to 50 copies:	$6.40 each + 10% postage and handling
51 and over:	$4.90 each + 10% postage and handling

Copies:_____ x Unit Price _____ = _____

2. Please rush me the following copies of *The Truth In Money Book:*

1 to 5 copies:	$14.95 each postpaid
6 to 51 copies:	$11.95 each + 10% postage and handling
52 (one case) and over	$ 8.95 each + 10% postage and handling

Copies:_____ x Unit Price _____ = _____

Total for books _____

10% for postage and handling as required _____

GRAND TOTAL _____

Thank you!

NAME _____

ADDRESS _____

CITY _____ STATE _____ ZIP _____

Please make check payable to Truth In Money, Inc.
Send to: Truth In Money, Inc., P. O. Box 30, Chagrin Falls, Ohio 44022